STICKEEN

Stickeen

John Muir (signature)

JOHN MUIR

with an afterword by
Malcolm Margolin

heyday books: berkeley

TEXT REPRINTED FROM THE
HOUGHTON MIFFLIN EDITION OF 1909
FRONT MATTER, AFTERWORD & CHRONOLOGY
DESIGNED BY
DAVID I. SHEIDLOWER

ISBN: 0-930588-05-3
L.C. CAT. CARD #: 81-81429
HEYDAY BOOKS
BOX 9145; BERKELEY, CALIFORNIA 94709
MUIR'S AUTOGRAPH APPEARS COURTESY OF
THE BANCROFT LIBRARY

CONTENTS

STICKEEN

IN the summer of 1880 I set out
from Fort Wrangel in a canoe to
continue the exploration of the icy
region of southeastern Alaska, be-
gun in the fall of 1879. After the
necessary provisions, blankets, etc.,
had been collected and stowed away,
and my Indian crew were in their
places ready to start, while a crowd
of their relatives and friends on the
wharf were bidding them good-by
and good-luck, my companion, the
Rev. S. H. Young, for whom we
were waiting, at last came aboard,
followed by a little black dog, that

Stickeen

immediately made himself at home by curling up in a hollow among the baggage. I like dogs, but this one seemed so small and worthless that I objected to his going, and asked the missionary why he was taking him.

" Such a little helpless creature will only be in the way," I said; "you had better pass him up to the Indian boys on the wharf, to be taken home to play with the children. This trip is not likely to be good for toy-dogs. The poor silly thing will be in rain and snow for weeks or months, and will require care like a baby."

But his master assured me that he would be no trouble at all; that he

Stickeen

was a perfect wonder of a dog, could
endure cold and hunger like a bear,
swim like a seal, and was wondrous
wise and cunning, etc., making out a
list of virtues to show he might be the
most interesting member of the party.

Nobody could hope to unravel the
lines of his ancestry. In all the wonderfully mixed and varied dog-tribe
I never saw any creature very much
like him, though in some of his sly,
soft, gliding motions and gestures
he brought the fox to mind. He was
short-legged and bunchy-bodied, and
his hair, though smooth, was long
and silky and slightly waved, so that
when the wind was at his back it ruf-

Stickeen

fled, making him look shaggy. At first sight his only noticeable feature was his fine tail, which was about as airy and shady as a squirrel's, and was carried curling forward almost to his nose. On closer inspection you might notice his thin sensitive ears, and sharp eyes with cunning tan-spots above them. Mr. Young told me that when the little fellow was a pup about the size of a woodrat he was presented to his wife by an Irish prospector at Sitka, and that on his arrival at Fort Wrangel he was adopted with enthusiasm by the Stickeen Indians as a sort of new good-luck totem, was named "Stickeen" for the tribe, and became

Stickeen

a universal favorite; petted, protected, and admired wherever he went, and regarded as a mysterious fountain of wisdom.

On our trip he soon proved himself a queer character — odd, concealed, independent, keeping invincibly quiet, and doing many little puzzling things that piqued my curiosity. As we sailed week after week through the long intricate channels and inlets among the innumerable islands and mountains of the coast, he spent most of the dull days in sluggish ease, motionless, and apparently as unobserving as if in deep sleep. But I discovered that somehow he always knew what was going on. When the Indians were about to shoot at ducks or seals, or when anything along the shore was exciting our attention, he would rest his chin on the edge of the canoe and calmly look out like a dreamy-eyed tourist. And when he heard us talking about making a landing, he immediately roused himself to see what sort of a place we were coming to, and made ready to jump overboard and swim ashore as soon as the canoe neared the beach. Then, with a vigorous shake to get rid of the brine in his hair, he ran into the woods to hunt small game. But though always the first out of the canoe, he was always the last to get

Stickeen

into it. When we were ready to start
he could never be found, and refused
to come to our call. We soon found
out, however, that though we could
not see him at such times, he saw us,
and from the cover of the briers and
huckleberry bushes in the fringe of
the woods was watching the canoe
with wary eye. For as soon as we were
fairly off he came trotting down the
beach, plunged into the surf, and swam
after us, knowing well that we would
cease rowing and take him in. When
the contrary little vagabond came
alongside, he was lifted by the neck,
held at arm's length a moment to drip,
and dropped aboard. We tried to cure

him of this trick by compelling him to swim a long way, as if we had a mind to abandon him; but this did no good: the longer the swim the better he seemed to like it.

Though capable of great idleness, he never failed to be ready for all sorts of adventures and excursions. One pitch - dark rainy night we landed about ten o'clock at the mouth of a salmon stream when the water was phosphorescent. The salmon were running, and the myriad fins of the onrushing multitude were churning all the stream into a silvery glow, wonderfully beautiful and impressive in the ebon darkness. To get a good

view of the show I set out with one of
the Indians and sailed up through the
midst of it to the foot of a rapid about
half a mile from camp, where the swift
current dashing over rocks made the
luminous glow most glorious. Hap-
pening to look back down the stream,
while the Indian was catching a few
of the struggling fish, I saw a long
spreading fan of light like the tail of
a comet, which we thought must be
made by some big strange animal that
was pursuing us. On it came with its
magnificent train, until we imagined
we could see the monster's head and
eyes; but it was only Stickeen, who,
finding I had left the camp, came

swimming after me to see what was up.

When we camped early, the best hunter of the crew usually went to the woods for a deer, and Stickeen was sure to be at his heels, provided I had not gone out. For, strange to say, though I never carried a gun, he always followed me, forsaking the hunter and even his master to share my wanderings. The days that were too stormy for sailing I spent in the woods, or on the adjacent mountains, wherever my studies called me; and Stickeen always insisted on going with me, however wild the weather, gliding like a fox through dripping huckleberry bushes and thorny tangles of panax and rubus, scarce stirring their rain-laden leaves; wading and wallowing through snow, swimming icy streams, skipping over logs and rocks and the crevasses of glaciers with the patience and endurance of a determined mountaineer, never tiring or getting discouraged. Once he followed me over a glacier the surface of which was so crusty and rough that it cut his feet until every step was marked with blood; but he trotted on with Indian fortitude until I noticed his red track, and, taking pity on him, made him a set of moccasins out of a handkerchief. However great his troubles he never asked help or made any complaint, as if, like a philosopher, he had learned that without hard work and suffering there could be no pleasure worth having.

Yet none of us was able to make out what Stickeen was really good for. He seemed to meet danger and hardships without anything like reason, insisted on having his own way, never obeyed an order, and the hunter could never set him on anything, or make him fetch the birds he shot. His equanimity was so steady it seemed due to want of feeling; ordinary storms were pleasures to him, and as for mere rain, he flourished in it like a vegetable.

Stickeen

No matter what advances you might make, scarce a glance or a tail-wag would you get for your pains. But though he was apparently as cold as a glacier and about as impervious to fun, I tried hard to make his acquaintance, guessing there must be something worth while hidden beneath so much courage, endurance, and love of wild-weathery adventure. No superannuated mastiff or bulldog grown old in office surpassed this fluffy midget in stoic dignity. He sometimes reminded me of a small, squat, unshakable desert cactus. For he never displayed a single trace of the merry, tricksy, elfish fun of the terriers and collies that we all know, nor of their touching affection and devotion. Like children, most small dogs beg to be loved and allowed to love; but Stickeen seemed a very Diogenes, asking only to be let alone: a true child of the wilderness, holding the even tenor of his hidden life with the silence and serenity of nature. His strength of character lay in his eyes. They looked as old as the hills, and as young, and as wild. I never tired of looking into them : it was like looking into a landscape; but they were small and rather deep-set, and had no explaining lines around them to give out particulars. I was accustomed to look into the faces

of plants and animals, and I watched
the little sphinx more and more keenly
as an interesting study. But there is
no estimating the wit and wisdom
concealed and latent in our lower fellow mortals until made manifest by
profound experiences; for it is through
suffering that dogs as well as saints
are developed and made perfect.

After we had explored the Sundum
and Tahkoo fiords and their glaciers,
we sailed through Stephen's Passage
into Lynn Canal and thence through
Icy Strait into Cross Sound, searching
for unexplored inlets leading toward
the great fountain ice-fields of the
Fairweather Range. Here, while the

tide was in our favor, we were accompanied by a fleet of icebergs drifting out to the ocean from Glacier Bay. Slowly we paddled around Vancouver's Point, Wimbleton, our frail canoe tossed like a feather on the massive heaving swells coming in past Cape Spenser. For miles the sound is bounded by precipitous mural cliffs, which, lashed with wave-spray and their heads hidden in clouds, looked terribly threatening and stern. Had our canoe been crushed or upset we could have made no landing here, for the cliffs, as high as those of Yosemite, sink sheer into deep water. Eagerly we scanned the wall on the north side

Stickeen

for the first sign of an opening fiord or harbor, all of us anxious except Stickeen, who dozed in peace or gazed dreamily at the tremendous precipices when he heard us talking about them. At length we made the joyful discovery of the mouth of the inlet now called "Taylor Bay," and about five o'clock reached the head of it and encamped in a spruce grove near the front of a large glacier.

While camp was being made, Joe the hunter climbed the mountain wall on the east side of the fiord in pursuit of wild goats, while Mr. Young and I went to the glacier. We found that it is separated from the waters of the inlet by a tide-washed moraine, and extends, an abrupt barrier, all the way across from wall to wall of the inlet, a distance of about three miles. But our most interesting discovery was that it had recently advanced, though again slightly receding. A portion of the terminal moraine had been plowed up and shoved forward, uprooting and overwhelming the woods on the east side. Many of the trees were down and buried, or nearly so, others were leaning away from the ice-cliffs, ready to fall, and some stood erect, with the bottom of the ice-plow still beneath their roots and its lofty crystal spires towering high above their tops. The spectacle presented by these century-old trees standing close beside a spiry wall of ice, with their branches almost touching it, was most novel and striking. And when I climbed around the front, and a little way up the west side of the glacier, I found that it had swelled and increased in height and width in accordance with its advance, and carried away the outer ranks of trees on its bank.

On our way back to camp after these first observations I planned a far-and-wide excursion for the morrow. I awoke early, called not only by the glacier, which had been on my mind all night, but by a grand flood-storm. The wind was blowing a gale from the north and the rain was flying with the clouds in a wide passionate horizontal flood, as if it were all passing over the country instead of falling on it. The main perennial streams were booming high above their banks, and hundreds of new ones, roaring like the sea, almost covered the lofty gray walls of the inlet with white cascades and falls. I had intended making a cup of coffee and getting something like a breakfast before starting, but when I heard the storm and looked out I made haste to join it; for many of Nature's finest lessons are to be found in her storms,

and if careful to keep in right rela-
tions with them, we may go safely
abroad with them, rejoicing in the
grandeur and beauty of their works
and ways, and chanting with the old
Norsemen, "The blast of the tem-
pest aids our oars, the hurricane is
our servant and drives us whither we
wish to go." So, omitting breakfast,
I put a piece of bread in my pocket
and hurried away.

Mr. Young and the Indians were
asleep, and so, I hoped, was Stickeen;
but I had not gone a dozen rods before
he left his bed in the tent and came
boring through the blast after me.
That a man should welcome storms

for their exhilarating music and motion, and go forth to see God making landscapes, is reasonable enough ; but what fascination could there be in such tremendous weather for a dog? Surely nothing akin to human enthusiasm for scenery or geology. Anyhow, on he came, breakfastless, through the choking blast. I stopped and did my best to turn him back. "Now don't," I said, shouting to make myself heard in the storm, "now don't, Stickeen. What has got into your queer noddle now? You must be daft. This wild day has nothing for you. There is no game abroad, nothing but weather. Go back to camp and keep warm, get a good breakfast with your master, and be sensible for once. I can't carry you all day or feed you, and this storm will kill you."

But Nature, it seems, was at the bottom of the affair, and she gains her ends with dogs as well as with men, making us do as she likes, shoving and pulling us along her ways, however rough, all but killing us at times in getting her lessons driven hard home. After I had stopped again and again, shouting good warning advice, I saw that he was not to be shaken off; as well might the earth try to shake off the moon. I had once led his master into trouble, when he fell on one of the topmost jags of a mountain and dislocated his arm; now the turn of his humble companion was coming. The pitiful little wanderer just stood there in the wind, drenched and blinking, saying doggedly, "Where thou goest I will go." So at last I told him to come on if he must, and gave him a piece of the bread I had in my pocket; then we struggled on together, and thus began the most memorable of all my wild days.

The level flood, driving hard in our faces, thrashed and washed us wildly until we got into the shelter of a grove on the east side of the glacier near the front, where we stopped awhile for breath and to listen and look out. The exploration of the glacier was my main object, but the wind was too high to allow excursions over its open surface, where one might be dangerously shoved while balancing for a jump on the brink of a crevasse. In the mean time the storm was a fine study. Here the end of the glacier, descending an abrupt swell of resisting rock about five hundred feet high, leans forward and falls in ice cascades. And as the storm came down the glacier from the North, Stickeen and I were beneath the main current of the blast, while favorably located to see and hear it. What a psalm the storm was singing, and how fresh the smell of the washed earth and leaves, and how sweet the still small voices of the storm! Detached wafts and swirls were coming through the woods, with music from the leaves and branches and furrowed boles, and even from the splintered rocks and ice-crags overhead, many of the tones soft and low and flute-like, as if each leaf and tree, crag and spire were a tuned reed. A broad torrent, draining the side of the glacier, now swollen by scores of new streams from the mountains, was rolling boulders along its rocky channel, with thudding, bumping, muffled sounds, rushing towards the bay with tremendous energy, as if in haste to get out of the mountains; the waters above and beneath calling to each other, and all to the ocean, their home.

Looking southward from our shelter, we had this great torrent and the forested mountain wall above it on our left, the spiry ice-crags on our right, and smooth gray gloom ahead. I tried to draw the marvelous scene in my note-book, but the rain blurred the page in spite of all my pains to shelter it, and the sketch was almost worthless. When the wind began to abate, I traced the east side of the glacier. All the trees standing on the edge of the woods were barked and bruised, showing high-ice mark in a very telling way, while tens of thousands of those that had stood for centuries on the bank of the glacier farther out lay crushed and being crushed. In many places I could see down fifty feet or so beneath the margin of the glacier-mill, where trunks from one to two feet in diameter were being ground to pulp against outstanding rock-ribs and bosses of the bank.

About three miles above the front of the glacier I climbed to the surface of it by means of axe-steps made easy for Stickeen. As far as the eye could reach, the level, or nearly level, gla-

cier stretched away indefinitely beneath the gray sky, a seemingly
boundless prairie of ice. The rain con-
tinued, and grew colder, which I did
not mind, but a dim snowy look in
the drooping clouds made me hesitate
about venturing far from land. No
trace of the west shore was visible,
and in case the clouds should settle
and give snow, or the wind again become violent, I feared getting caught
in a tangle of crevasses. Snow-crys-
tals, the flowers of the mountain
clouds, are frail, beautiful things, but
terrible when flying on storm-winds
in darkening, benumbing swarms, or,
when welded together into glaciers

full of deadly crevasses. Watching the weather, I sauntered about on the crystal sea. For a mile or two out I found the ice remarkably safe. The marginal crevasses were mostly narrow, while the few wider ones were easily avoided by passing around them, and the clouds began to open here and there.

Thus encouraged, I at last pushed out for the other side; for Nature can make us do anything she likes. At first we made rapid progress, and the sky was not very threatening, while I took bearings occasionally with a pocket compass to enable me to find my way back more surely in case the storm should become blinding; but the structure lines of the glacier were my main guide. Toward the west side we came to a closely crevassed section in which we had to make long, narrow tacks and doublings, tracing the edges of tremendous transverse and longitudinal crevasses, many of which were from twenty to thirty feet wide, and perhaps a thousand feet deep — beautiful and awful. In working a way through them I was severely cautious, but Stickeen came on as unhesitating as the flying clouds. The widest crevasse that I could jump he would leap without so much as halting to take a look at it. The weather was now making quick changes, scattering bits of dazzling brightness through the wintry gloom; at rare intervals, when the sun broke forth wholly free, the glacier was seen from shore to shore with a bright array of encompassing mountains partly revealed, wearing the clouds as garments, while the prairie bloomed and sparkled with irised light from myriads of washed crystals. Then suddenly all the glorious show would be darkened and blotted out.

Stickeen seemed to care for none of these things, bright or dark, nor for the crevasses, wells, moulins, or swift flashing streams into which he

might fall. The little adventurer was
only about two years old, yet nothing seemed novel to him, nothing
daunted him. He showed neither cau-
tion nor curiosity, wonder nor fear,
but bravely trotted on as if glaciers
were playgrounds. His stout, muffled body seemed all one skipping
muscle, and it was truly wonderful to
see how swiftly and to all appearance
heedlessly he flashed across nerve-
trying chasms six or eight feet wide.
His courage was so unwavering that
it seemed to be due to dullness of
perception, as if he were only blindly
bold; and I kept warning him to be
careful. For we had been close com-

panions on so many wilderness trips
that I had formed the habit of talking
to him as if he were a boy and under-
stood every word.

We gained the west shore in about
three hours; the width of the glacier
here being about seven miles. Then I
pushed northward in order to see as
far back as possible into the fountains
of the Fairweather Mountains, in case
the clouds should rise. The walking
was easy along the margin of the
forest, which, of course, like that on
the other side, had been invaded and
crushed by the swollen, overflowing
glacier. In an hour or so, after passing a massive headland, we came

suddenly on a branch of the glacier, which, in the form of a magnificent ice-cascade two miles wide, was pouring over the rim of the main basin in a westerly direction, its surface broken into wave-shaped blades and shattered blocks, suggesting the wildest updashing, heaving, plunging motion of a great river cataract. Tracing it down three or four miles, I found that it discharged into a lake, filling it with icebergs.

I would gladly have followed the lake outlet to tide-water, but the day was already far spent, and the threatening sky called for haste on the return trip to get off the ice before dark.

Stickeen

I decided therefore to go no farther,
and, after taking a general view of the
wonderful region, turned back, hoping to see it again under more favor-
able auspices. We made good speed
up the cañon of the great ice-torrent,
and out on the main glacier until we
had left the west shore about two
miles behind us. Here we got into a
difficult network of crevasses, the
gathering clouds began to drop misty
fringes, and soon the dreaded snow
came flying thick and fast. I now
began to feel anxious about finding a
way in the blurring storm. Stickeen
showed no trace of fear. He was still
the same silent, able little hero. I no-

ticed, however, that after the storm-darkness came on he kept close up behind me. The snow urged us to make still greater haste, but at the same time hid our way. I pushed on as best I could, jumping innumerable crevasses, and for every hundred rods or so of direct advance traveling a mile in doubling up and down in the turmoil of chasms and dislocated ice-blocks. After an hour or two of this work we came to a series of longi-tudinal crevasses of appalling width, and almost straight and regular in trend, like immense furrows. These I traced with firm nerve, excited and strengthened by the danger, making wide jumps, poising cautiously on their dizzy edges after cutting hollows for my feet before making the spring, to avoid possible slipping or any uncertainty on the farther sides, where only one trial is granted — exercise at once frightful and inspiring. Stickeen followed seemingly without effort.

Many a mile we thus traveled, mostly up and down, making but little real headway in crossing, running instead of walking most of the time as the danger of being compelled to spend the night on the glacier became threatening. Stickeen seemed able for anything. Doubtless we could have weathered the storm for one night, dancing on a flat spot to keep from freezing, and I faced the threat without feeling anything like despair; but we were hungry and wet, and the wind from the mountains was still thick with snow and bitterly cold, so of course that night would have seemed a very long one. I could not see far enough through the blurring snow to judge in which general direction the least dangerous route lay, while the few dim, momentary glimpses I caught of mountains through rifts in the flying clouds were far from encouraging either as weather signs or as guides. I had simply to grope my way from crevasse to crevasse, holding a general direction by the ice-structure, which was not to be seen everywhere, and partly by the wind. Again and again I was put to my mettle, but Stickeen followed easily, his nerve apparently growing more unflinching as the danger increased. So it always is with mountaineers when hard beset. Running hard and jumping, holding every minute of the remaining daylight, poor as it was, precious, we doggedly persevered and tried to hope that every difficult crevasse we overcame would prove to be the last of its kind. But on the contrary, as we advanced they became more deadly trying.

At length our way was barred by a very wide and straight crevasse, which I traced rapidly northward a mile or so without finding a crossing or hope of one; then down the glacier about as far, to where it united with another uncrossable crevasse. In all this distance of perhaps two miles there was only one place where I could possibly jump it, but the width of this jump was the utmost I dared attempt, while the danger of slipping on the farther side was so great that I was loath to try it. Furthermore, the side I was on was about a foot higher than the other, and even with this advantage the crevasse seemed dangerously wide. One is liable to underestimate the width of crevasses where the magnitudes in general are great. I therefore stared at this one mighty keenly, estimating its width and the shape of the edge on the farther side, until I thought that I could jump it if necessary, but that in case I should be compelled to jump back from the lower side I might fail. Now, a cautious mountaineer seldom takes a step on unknown ground which seems at all dangerous that he cannot retrace in case he should be stopped by unseen obstacles ahead. This is the rule of mountaineers who live long, and, though in haste, I compelled myself to sit down and calmly deliberate before I broke it.

Retracing my devious path in imagination as if it were drawn on a chart, I saw that I was recrossing the glacier a mile or two farther up stream than the course pursued in the morning, and that I was now entangled in a section I had not before seen. Should I risk this dangerous jump, or try to regain the woods on the west shore, make a fire, and have only hunger to endure while waiting for a new day? I had already crossed so broad a stretch of dangerous ice that

Stickeen

I saw it would be difficult to get back to the woods through the storm, before dark, and the attempt would most likely result in a dismal night-dance on the glacier; while just beyond the present barrier the surface seemed more promising, and the east shore was now perhaps about as near as the west. I was therefore eager to go on. But this wide jump was a dreadful obstacle.

At length, because of the dangers already behind me, I determined to venture against those that might be ahead, jumped and landed well, but with so little to spare that I more than ever dreaded being compelled to take

that jump back from the lower side.
Stickeen followed, making nothing of
it, and we ran eagerly forward, hoping we were leaving all our troubles
behind. But within the distance of a
few hundred yards we were stopped by
the widest crevasse yet encountered.
Of course I made haste to explore it,
hoping all might yet be remedied
by finding a bridge or a way around
either end. About three-fourths of a
mile upstream I found that it united
with the one we had just crossed, as
I feared it would. Then, tracing it
down, I found it joined the same crevasse at the lower end also, maintain-
ing throughout its whole course a

width of forty to fifty feet. Thus to my dismay I discovered that we were on a narrow island about two miles long, with two barely possible ways of escape : one back by the way we came, the other ahead by an almost inaccessible sliver-bridge that crossed the great crevasse from near the middle of it!

After this nerve-trying discovery I ran back to the sliver-bridge and cautiously examined it. Crevasses, caused by strains from variations in the rate of motion of different parts of the glacier and convexities in the channel, are mere cracks when they first open, so narrow as hardly to admit the blade of a pocket-knife, and gradually widen according to the extent of the strain and the depth of the glacier. Now some of these cracks are interrupted, like the cracks in wood, and in opening, the strip of ice between overlapping ends is dragged out, and may maintain a continuous connection between the sides, just as the two sides of a slivered crack in wood that is being split are connected. Some crevasses remain open for months or even years, and by the melting of their sides continue to increase in width long after the opening strain has ceased; while the sliver-bridges, level on top at first and perfectly safe, are at length melted to thin, vertical, knife-edged blades, the upper portion being most exposed to the weather; and since the exposure is greatest in the middle, they at length curve downward like the cables of suspension bridges. This one was evidently very old, for it had been weathered and wasted until it was the most dangerous and inaccessible that ever lay in my way. The width of the crevasse was here about fifty feet, and the sliver crossing diagonally was about seventy feet long; its thin knife-edge near the middle was depressed twenty-five or thirty feet below the level of the glacier, and the upcurving

ends were attached to the sides eight
or ten feet below the brink. Getting
down the nearly vertical wall to the
end of the sliver and up the other side
were the main difficulties, and they
seemed all but insurmountable. Of the
many perils encountered in my years
of wandering on mountains and glaciers none seemed so plain and stern
and merciless as this. And it was presented when we were wet to the skin
and hungry, the sky dark with quick
driving snow, and the night near.
But we were forced to face it. It was
a tremendous necessity.

Beginning, not immediately above
the sunken end of the bridge, but a

little to one side, I cut a deep hollow on the brink for my knees to rest in. Then, leaning over, with my short-handled axe I cut a step sixteen or eighteen inches below, which on account of the sheerness of the wall was necessarily shallow. That step, how-ever, was well made; its floor sloped slightly inward and formed a good hold for my heels. Then, slipping cautiously upon it, and crouching as low as possible, with my left side toward the wall, I steadied myself against the wind with my left hand in a slight notch, while with the right I cut other similar steps and notches in succession, guarding against losing balance by glinting of the axe, or by wind-gusts, for life and death were in every stroke and in the niceness of finish of every foothold.

After the end of the bridge was reached I chipped it down until I had made a level platform six or eight inches wide, and it was a trying thing to poise on this little slippery platform while bending over to get safely astride of the sliver. Crossing was then comparatively easy by chipping off the sharp edge with short, careful strokes, and hitching forward an inch or two at a time, keeping my balance with my knees pressed against the sides. The tremendous abyss on either hand I studiously ignored. To me the edge of that blue sliver was then all the world. But the most trying part of the adventure, after working my way across inch by inch and chipping another small platform, was to rise from the safe position astride and to cut a step-ladder in the nearly vertical face of the wall, — chipping, climbing, holding on with feet and fingers in mere notches. At such times one's whole body is eye, and common skill and fortitude are replaced by power beyond our call or knowledge. Never before had I been so long under deadly strain. How I got up that cliff I never could tell. The thing seemed

to have been done by somebody else.
I never have held death in contempt,
though in the course of my explora-
tions I have oftentimes felt that to
meet one's fate on a noble mountain,
or in the heart of a glacier, would be
blessed as compared with death from
disease, or from some shabby lowland
accident. But the best death, quick and
crystal-pure, set so glaringly open before us, is hard enough to face, even
though we feel gratefully sure that
we have already had happiness enough
for a dozen lives.

But poor Stickeen, the wee, hairy,
sleekit beastie, think of him! When I
had decided to dare the bridge, and

while I was on my knees chipping a hollow on the rounded brow above it, he came behind me, pushed his head past my shoulder, looked down and across, scanned the sliver and its approaches with his mysterious eyes, then looked me in the face with a startled air of surprise and concern, and began to mutter and whine; saying as plainly as if speaking with words, "Surely, you are not going into that awful place." This was the first time I had seen him gaze deliberately into a crevasse, or into my face with an eager, speaking, troubled look. That he should have recognized and appreciated the danger at the first glance showed wonderful sagacity. Never before had the daring midget seemed to know that ice was slippery or that there was any such thing as danger anywhere. His looks and tones of voice when he began to complain and speak his fears were so human that I unconsciously talked to him in sympathy as I would to a frightened boy, and in trying to calm his fears perhaps in some measure moderated my own. "Hush your fears, my boy," I said, "we will get across safe, though it is not going to be easy. No right way is easy in this rough world. We must risk our lives to save them. At the worst we can only slip, and then how grand a grave we will have, and by and by our nice bones will do good in the terminal moraine."

But my sermon was far from reassuring him: he began to cry, and after taking another piercing look at the tremendous gulf, ran away in desperate excitement, seeking some other crossing. By the time he got back, baffled of course, I had made a step or two. I dared not look back, but he made himself heard; and when he saw that I was certainly bent on crossing he cried aloud in despair. The danger was enough to daunt anybody, but it seems wonderful that he should have been able to weigh and appreciate it so justly. No mountaineer could have seen it more quickly or judged it more wisely, discriminating between real and apparent peril.

When I gained the other side, he screamed louder than ever, and after running back and forth in vain search for a way of escape, he would return to the brink of the crevasse above the bridge, moaning and wailing as if in the bitterness of death. Could this be the silent, philosophic Stickeen? I shouted encouragement, telling him the bridge was not so bad as it looked, that I had left it flat and safe for his feet, and he could walk it easily. But he was afraid to try. Strange so small an animal should be capable of such big, wise fears. I called again and again in a reassuring tone to come on and fear nothing; that he could come if he would only try. He would hush for a moment, look down again at the bridge, and shout his unshakable conviction that he could never, never come that way; then lie back in despair, as if howling, "O-o-oh! what a place! No-o-o, I can never go-o-o down there!" His natural composure and courage had vanished utterly in a tumultuous storm of fear. Had the danger been less, his distress would have seemed ridiculous. But in this dismal, merciless abyss lay the shadow of death, and his heartrending cries might well have called Heaven to his help. Perhaps they did. So hidden before, he was now transparent, and one could see the workings of his heart and mind like the movements of a clock out of its case. His voice and gestures, hopes and fears, were so perfectly human that none could mistake them; while he seemed to understand every word of mine. I was troubled at the thought of having to leave him out all night, and of the danger of not finding him in the morning. It seemed impossible to get him to venture. To compel him to try

through fear of being abandoned, I
started off as if leaving him to his fate,
and disappeared back of a hummock;
but this did no good; he only lay down
and moaned in utter hopeless misery.
So, after hiding a few minutes, I went
back to the brink of the crevasse and in
a severe tone of voice shouted across
to him that now I must certainly leave
him, I could wait no longer, and that,
if he would not come, all I could pro-
mise was that I would return to seek
him next day. I warned him that if he
went back to the woods the wolves
would kill him, and finished by urg-
ing him once more by words and gestures to come on, come on.

Stickeen

He knew very well what I meant, and at last, with the courage of despair, hushed and breathless, he crouched down on the brink in the hollow I had made for my knees, pressed his body against the ice as if trying to get the advantage of the friction of every hair, gazed into the first step, put his little feet together and slid them slowly, slowly over the edge and down into it, bunching all four in it and almost standing on his head. Then, without lifting his feet, as well as I could see through the snow, he slowly worked them over the edge of the step and down into the next and the next in succession in the

same way, and gained the end of
the bridge. Then, lifting his feet with
the regularity and slowness of the
vibrations of a seconds pendulum, as
if counting and measuring *one-two-
three*, holding himself steady against
the gusty wind, and giving separate
attention to each little step, he gained
the foot of the cliff, while I was on my
knees leaning over to give him a lift
should he succeed in getting within
reach of my arm. Here he halted in
dead silence, and it was here I feared
he might fail, for dogs are poor climb-
ers. I had no cord. If I had had one,
I would have dropped a noose over
his head and hauled him up. But while

Stickeen

I was thinking whether an available cord might be made out of clothing, he was looking keenly into the series of notched steps and finger-holds I had made, as if counting them, and fixing the position of each one of them in his mind. Then suddenly up he came in a springy rush, hooking his paws into the steps and notches so quickly that I could not see how it was done, and whizzed past my head, safe at last!

And now came a scene! "Well done, well done, little boy! Brave boy!" I cried, trying to catch and caress him; but he would not be caught. Never before or since have I seen anything like so passionate a revulsion from the depths of despair to exultant, triumphant, uncontrollable joy. He flashed and darted hither and thither as if fairly demented, screaming and shouting, swirling round and round in giddy loops and circles like a leaf in a whirlwind, lying down, and rolling over and over, sidewise and heels over head, and pouring forth a tumultuous flood of hysterical cries and sobs and gasping mutterings. When I ran up to him to shake him, fearing he might die of joy, he flashed off two or three hundred yards, his feet in a mist of motion; then, turning suddenly, came back in a wild rush and launched himself at my face, almost knocking me down, all the time screeching and screaming and shouting as if saying, "Saved! saved! saved!" Then away again, dropping suddenly at times with his feet in the air, trembling and fairly sobbing. Such passionate emotion was enough to kill him. Moses' stately song of triumph after escaping the Egyptians and the Red Sea was nothing to it. Who could have guessed the capacity of the dull, enduring little fellow for all that most stirs this mortal frame? Nobody could have helped crying with him!

But there is nothing like work for

toning down excessive fear or joy.
So I ran ahead, calling him in as
gruff a voice as I could command to
come on and stop his nonsense, for
we had far to go and it would soon be
dark. Neither of us feared another
trial like this. Heaven would surely
count one enough for a lifetime. The
ice ahead was gashed by thousands
of crevasses, but they were common
ones. The joy of deliverance burned
in us like fire, and we ran without
fatigue, every muscle with immense
rebound glorying in its strength.
Stickeen flew across everything in
his way, and not till dark did he settle into his normal fox-like trot. At

Stickeen

last the cloudy mountains came in sight, and we soon felt the solid rock beneath our feet, and were safe. Then came weakness. Danger had vanished, and so had our strength. We tottered down the lateral moraine in the dark, over boulders and tree trunks, through the bushes and devil-club thickets of the grove where we had sheltered ourselves in the morning, and across the level mud-slope of the terminal moraine. We reached camp about ten o'clock, and found a big fire and a big supper. A party of Hoona Indians had visited Mr. Young, bringing a gift of porpoise meat and wild strawberries, and Hunter Joe had brought in a wild goat. But we lay down, too tired to eat much, and soon fell into a troubled sleep. The man who said, "The harder the toil, the sweeter the rest," never was profoundly tired. Stickeen kept springing up and muttering in his sleep, no doubt dreaming that he was still on the brink of the crevasse; and so did I, that night and many others long afterward, when I was overtired.

Thereafter Stickeen was a changed dog. During the rest of the trip, instead of holding aloof, he always lay by my side, tried to keep me constantly in sight, and would hardly

accept a morsel of food, however
tempting, from any hand but mine.
At night, when all was quiet about
the camp-fire, he would come to me
and rest his head on my knee with a
look of devotion as if I were his god.
And often as he caught my eye he
seemed to be trying to say, " Was
n't that an awful time we had together on the glacier?"

Nothing in after years has dimmed
that Alaska storm-day. As I write it
all comes rushing and roaring to
mind as if I were again in the heart
of it. Again I see the gray flying
clouds with their rain-floods and

snow, the ice-cliffs towering above
the shrinking forest, the majestic ice-
cascade, the vast glacier outspread
before its white mountain fountains,
and in the heart of it the tremendous
crevasse,—emblem of the valley of
the shadow of death,—low clouds
trailing over it, the snow falling into
it; and on its brink I see little Stickeen, and I hear his cries for help and
his shouts of joy. I have known many
dogs, and many a story I could tell
of their wisdom and devotion; but to
none do I owe so much as to Stickeen. At first the least promising and
least known of my dog-friends, he
suddenly became the best known of

Stickeen

them all. Our storm-battle for life brought him to light, and through him as through a window I have ever since been looking with deeper sympathy into all my fellow mortals.

None of Stickeen's friends knows what finally became of him. After my work for the season was done I departed for California, and I never saw the dear little fellow again. In reply to anxious inquiries his master wrote me that in the summer of 1883 he was stolen by a tourist at Fort Wrangel and taken away on a steamer. His fate is wrapped in mystery. Doubtless he has left this

Stickeen

world — crossed the last crevasse — and gone to another. But he will not be forgotten. To me Stickeen is immortal.

Afterword

JOHN MUIR met the Reverend S. Hall Young for the first time in the summer of 1879, a year before the adventure with Stickeen. Young, a missionary among the Tlinget Indians, describes Muir among the passengers arriving at Fort Wrangell, Alaska: "Standing a little apart from them as the steamboat drew to the dock, his peering blue eyes already eagerly scanning the islands and mountains, was a lean, sinewy man of forty, with waving, reddish-brown hair and beard, and shoulders slightly stooped. He wore a Scotch cap and a long, gray tweed ulster, which I have always since associated with him."

A strong and immediate friendship grew up between John Muir and the Reverend Young, and shortly after their first meeting they took off together for a day of mountain climbing. To climb with Muir was an experience no one ever forgot. Young described it in his book, *Alaska Days With John Muir*: "There was never an instant when both feet and hands were not in play, and often elbows, knees, thighs, upper arms, and even chin must grip and hold. Clambering up a steep slope... pulling up smooth rock-faces by sheer strength of arm and chinning over the edge, leaping fissures, sliding flat around a dangerous rock-breast, testing crumbling spurs before risking his weight, always going up, up, no hesitation, no pause—that was Muir!"

Young struggled to keep pace. In years past he had repeatedly dislocated both arms, and as he pulled himself up he felt the strain on his sockets. But, eager to impress Muir and keep up with him, he said nothing. On the descent, however, Young slipped, and as he reached out to catch himself both arms came entirely out of their joints. His arms useless and paralyzed, he slid down the rubble slope toward a cliff and a thousand-foot drop to a glacier below. He stopped at the very rim, his legs reaching out into the void.

"Grab that rock, man, just by your right hand," yelled Muir.

"My arms are out," Young gurgled desperately.

There was a pause. Then Muir's voice rang out, cheery and full of confidence: "Hold fast; I'm going to get you out of this." Muir began whistling and singing snatches of Scottish songs, calling his encouragement to Young. Young hung on—he never knew how—making his body as flat and heavy as possible, afraid even to twitch a muscle, wink an eyelid, or take a deep breath. Muir could not descend directly to where Young lay, but had to go along the slope and work his way back along the cliff edge—his foot-hold a precarious two-inch shelf. Upon reaching Young he grabbed him firmly and started back along the narrow shelf. Muir would pull Young toward him, set him in place, move a few inches, and then pull Young toward him again. In one place, needing his arms as well as his legs for support, he caught Young's collar in his teeth and holding him as a "panther with her cub" he climbed straight up a rock wall ten or twelve feet.

"It was utterly impossible," said Young, "Yet he did it!" Throughout the long night Muir carried and led the crippled Young down the mountain to help.

Young's arms were later pulled back into their sockets and he recovered rapidly. Although he never went climbing high peaks with Muir again, their friendship deepened. In October and November of that year they set off in an open canoe with a native crew to explore the Alexander Archipelago, a group of some eleven hundred wooded islands—Young to proselytize the Indians who had never before seen a missionary; Muir to study living glaciers, to botanize, and of course to exult in the beauties and mysteries of the world. The trip was true exploration. Alaska was then a frontier, purchased from Russia only a dozen years before. Its coast was largely uncharted, its interior almost entirely unknown. Alaska was a large blank area on the maps of the world. In their open, red-cedar canoe Young and Muir visited bays and penetrated fjords for the first time on record. A major discovery of the trip was Glacier Bay and the immense ice-river that later came to be called Muir

Glacier. They also caught a tantalizing glimpse of Taylor Bay and the Taylor Glacier before being beaten back by weather—a glimpse that was to haunt Muir all the next winter.

Muir returned to the San Francisco Bay Area in December, and the next April, when he was nearly forty-two years old, he married Louie Wanda Strentzel. A few months later he once again boarded a boat and arrived in Alaska.

"Where's your wife?" asked a surprised Reverend Young.

"Man," exclaimed Muir, "have you forgotten? Don't you know we lost a glacier last fall?... Get your canoe and crew and let us be off!"

Thus began the voyage immortalized by the presence of Stickeen.

One hates to comment directly on the story of *Stickeen*; it is so perfect and exultant a story that one fears any additional words would merely diminish it. But perhaps it would be useful to explain aspects of the story that might have been more obvious to a nineteenth century reader than to one of today.

First was Muir's fascination with glaciers. In the ten years before his Alaska trips Muir lived and worked in the High Sierra, and as he studied its carved and scoured valleys, he became fairly obsessed with the action of glaciers in ages past. "The grandeur of these forces and their glorious results overpower me and inhabit my whole being. Waking or sleeping I have no rest. In dreams I read blurred sheets of glacial writing, or follow lines of cleavage, or struggle with the difficulties of some extraordinary rock-form.''

After an outing in 1879 on what was later to be called Muir Glacier, he returned to Young in a state of ecstacy: ''Man, man; you ought to have been with me. You'll never make up what you lost today. I've been wandering through a thousand rooms of God's crystal temple. I've been a thousand feet down in the crevasses, with matchless domes and sculptured figures and carved ice-work all about me. Solomon's marble and ivory palaces were nothing to it. Such purity, such color, such delicate beauty! I was tempted to stay there and feast my soul, and softly freeze, until I would become part of the glacier. What a great death that would be!''

In the nineteenth century, when geology was still a new and controversial science, glacier-study was an exciting, even urgent, pursuit. Scholars were just breaking away from the biblical interpretation of creation: that the world had been made in six days and that it was no more than about 5,000 or 6,000 years old. The idea that portions of the Northern Hemisphere had once been covered by glaciers, and that these glaciers—not the direct hand of God—had gouged valleys, polished granite, and shaped mountains, burst upon educated people everywhere with tremendous force. Such an idea demanded a different understanding of landscape, a different sense of time and scale, a new *Genesis*.

Muir was considered by many people of his age, the famed geologist John Tyndall among them, to have been the world's foremost expert on glaciers. In the Sierra he could study the effects of ancient glaciers; but in Alaska he could measure glacial movements, hear the grinding, and see with his own eyes the workings of "God's plow." Here he could "learn many new and wonderful facts about world-shaping;" here he could stand witness to the ongoing creation of the world.

Muir called his adventure with Stickeen "the most memorable of all my wild days." It was an experience that stayed with him throughout his life and shaped his thinking. Until his death at the age of seventy-six, Muir talked frequently of the little dog. He filled a large notebook with his thoughts about their day on the glacier, and he wrote many comments about it in the flyleaves of other books he owned. He told the story of Stickeen again and again. At parties or lectures it was said that waiters, porters, and servants would hide behind curtains or even under tables just to hear him tell the story.

For modern readers, *Stickeen* is pure tonic—

bracing, refreshing, a charge of affirmation and joy. But for Muir that day on the glacier was also a revelation, presenting him with a piece of irreducible knowledge that was to change his very understanding of the world. Animal life was not highly regarded in the nineteenth century. Most biblical adherents held that animals lacked true intelligence, passion, and above all souls; animals had been placed on earth to fill people's needs. Advanced scientists of that day also diminished animals, holding them capable only of mechanical, instinctual responses to their environments. They too felt that humans alone had real understanding and passion, humans alone were capable of original thought.

Stickeen, however, revealed a different truth. It was if the dog—driven to its utmost limits that day on the glacier—became momentarily transparent; and when Muir looked through to the essence of its being, what he saw in Stickeen was not very different from what he saw in himself. He and the dog were brothers, made of much the same stuff, differing from each other only in degree. "He enlarged my life," Muir wrote, "extended its boundaries... In all my wild walks seldom have I ever had a more definite and useful message to bring back. Stickeen was the herald of a new gospel." It was a gospel that Muir was to preach ardently the rest of his life, one that proclaimed the fundamental unity and sanctity of all living things.

Chronology of Muir's Life

1838— Born April 21 in Dunbar, Scotland; the third child and first son of a family of eight children.

1849— Family migrates to America and settles at Fountain Lake, Wisconsin, at that time the edge of wilderness.

1860— Gains local renown as an inventor of ingenious mechanical devices. Enters the University of Wisconsin at Madison.

1864— Makes a geological and botanical "tramp" around the Great Lakes and into Canada.

1865–66— Works in shops and factories, inventing and redesigning machinery, "busy almost to craziness...inventing machinery twenty-four hours a day."

1867— Undertakes "a thousand mile walk" from Kentucky through the war-ravaged south to Florida's Cedar Keyes, then on to Cuba.

1868— Arrives by boat in San Francisco, California, and immediately heads to the Sierra Nevada.

1869–72— Lives in Yosemite Valley, working first as a sheepherder in the high meadows, later as a sawyer in a Valley sawmill.

1873-76— Lives in Oakland and San Francisco. Begins writing articles about the geology and botany of the Sierra, frequently revisiting the mountains.

1877— Excursion to Utah in the spring. Then to Mount Shasta in late summer with botanists Joseph Hooker and Asa Gray. Muir returns to the San Francisco Bay area by canoeing down the Sacramento River.

1878— Employed by the U.S. Coast and Geodetic Survey to help survey parts of Nevada and Utah.

1879— First trip to Alaska. Discovers Glacier Bay.

1880— Marries Louie Wanda Strentzel. Returns to Alaska, and the adventure with Stickeen.

1881— Daughter, Anna Wanda, born. Muir joins an expedition to Alaska to search for the missing steamer, *Jeannette.*

1882— Begins actively managing the orchards of the Strentzel Ranch in Alhambra Valley, east of San Francisco Bay. Ranch business will absorb much of his energy for the next ten years.

1886— Second daughter, Helen, born. Travels with the artist, William Keith, to Vancouver, Puget Sound, and Mount Rainier.

1889— Becomes increasingly active in attempts to preserve the Sierra from overgrazing and logging, and to establish Yosemite Valley as a National Park.

1890— Another trip to Alaska.

1892— Leads in founding the Sierra Club, serving as president for the remainder of his life.

1893— Travels to the eastern United States and to Europe.

1894— First major book, *Mountains of California,* published.

1896— Serves as an advisor to the commission that will review forest lands throughout the country and recommend to Congress the formation of forest reserves.

1897— ''Stickeen'' is first published as a story in *Century Magazine.*

1899— Joins John Burroughs, C. Hart Merriam, and other naturalists on a trip to Alaska sponsored by E. H. Harriman.

1903— Camps for three days in Yosemite Valley with Theodore Roosevelt. Two years later Roosevelt will establish Yosemite as a National Park.

Travels to Europe, Siberia, Japan, China, India, and Australia.

1905— Wife dies. While visiting his daughter in the desert, he discovers the *Blue Forest* of petrified wood in Arizona.

1906— Instrumental in extending National Monument status to petrified forests.

1908— President Roosevelt sets aside a portion of the Grand Canyon as a National Monument, partly on Muir's recommendation. Muir becomes heavily involved in the attempt to save Hetch Hetchy Valley from flooding by a reservoir.

1909— *Stickeen* is first published in book form.

1911— Travels to South America and discovers groves of ''monkey puzzle'' trees in the Andes. Publication of *My First Summer in the Sierra.*

1912— Travels through Africa. Publication of *The Yosemite.*

1913— The Hetch Hetchy battle is lost. Publication of *Story of my Boyhood and Youth.*

1914— On Christmas Eve, John Muir dies. Manuscript pages of *Travels in Alaska* are scattered about his bed. Toward the end of his life he wrote on a scrap of paper: "Death is a kind of nurse saying, 'Come, children, to bed and get up in the morning,' —a gracious Mother calling her children home."